Advance Praise for I Choose...
A Journal to Rewire Your
Subconscious with Total Ease

The *I Choose...* Journal is the very thing you need to help turn your life around! The simple yet profound journaling exercises in this book will help you harness the energy of the powerful Universal Law of Attraction, setting it to work to bring all of your deepest, truest, most heartfelt desires to light. Your only job is to grab a pen, sit back, relax, feel good, and enjoy filling the pages with your intentions. Then wait to see your wishes unfold as they materialize before your eyes! Yes, life really *can* be that simple if you allow it. Joseph's journal will help guide you there.

—Dr. Ashleigh Stewart, Msc.D, Founder of the I AM
Abundance Academy, and Author of *5 Minutes to Mindfulness—
Kids*, and *How's the Weather Today?—My Feelings Forecast*

We can rewire our brain! By sending new signals to the brain that are positive and evoke positive feelings, we can change the negative, stressful fight-flight responses our bodies produce when past stress memories are triggered. By repetitive stimulation of positive input, neural synapses will strengthen the new signal, and the chemical connection between neurons firing stress reactions will become weaker. With the use of positive affirmations, we can create new circuits in our brain. Joseph P. Ghabi's book is a wonderful way to support you in rewiring your brain and creating new pathways for a happy new you.

—Dr. Christina Clapham, www.Alignmentforlife.ca

Joseph P. Ghabi, my profound mentor, invited me to use the exercise he created and calls the "I choose" method. It's a simple yet highly effective technique which created astonishing results! Prior to using this, my life was like riding a horse without reins down a narrow path along jagged cliffs in the dark with just the dimmest of lights for illumination. Joseph's suggestion placed the drooping reins gently back into my hands, helping me face everything and become the director of my own journey. Try it for yourself and see how quickly your life will change exponentially, for *your own* greater good and for all those who are part of your precious life!

—Deb English, Parksville BC

I CHOOSE...

A Journal to Rewire Your Subconscious With Total Ease

Dear Deb.
It is great to cross our
path.
Wishing all success
you deserve and a
smooth transition
into 5D consciousness
In light
LOVE
Joseph

Joseph P. Ghabi

Soul Vision Awakening

Welcome to your "I Choose" Journal

Congratulations for taking the first step in choosing to use this journal! Your well-thought-out decision will be very rewarding in your personal growth journey.

Let me introduce myself. My name is Joseph P. Ghabi. I was guided to move to the United States to study Electrical Engineering, and then I continued on and did my master's in Computer Science. Fortunately, I discovered that continuing on that path was not for me, so three months after my graduation, I decided to quit that career. I moved from New York City to Montreal, Canada. I didn't have a clue where it would take me. Where would this abrupt change lead me? One thing I admit is that I trust the hunches and feelings I always get regarding whether I'm in the right place or not. I've never questioned, overanalyzed, or even doubted them. In Montreal, I was introduced to meditation and Numerology. I was still confused about my direction and purpose in life, but I never put any obstacles in front of myself. I allowed my curiosity to explore, never making any excuses for myself. I kept an open mind even though I was trained to have a logical mind.

I ended up taking a course in electronic repair so I could open a business repairing TVs, VCRs, microwaves, etc. It helped me to make a little bit of money initially, and as it turned out, it's the foundation of what I do today. From Electrical Engineering I learned about energy, vibration, and frequency, and that's what I use today with my Blueprint Numerology.

If you want to find the secrets of the universe,
think in terms of energy, frequency and vibration.
~ Nikola Tesla

What I learned from Computer Science is programming, reprogramming, and changing command codes, and that is what I use in my healing work to reprogram the subconscious.

One day, I woke up with a memory of the time I was repairing a TV ...

When you burn out a fuse, most of the time the problem does not originate with the fuse. Something else on the circuit board is short-circuiting, which blows out the fuse (so as not to burn out the whole circuit board). If we keep changing the fuse over and over, and it keeps blowing, this could damage the entire circuit board. So it becomes important to look at what else could be short-circuiting the fuse. It could be a capacitor, a resistor, a chip, or the line that connects all the components. When I repaired a burned-out circuit board, I needed to create a new pathway, as the old pathway was no longer repairable. Sometimes with blown fuses, the socket of a resistor or a capacitor is no longer fit to use, so I'd have to use an outside wire and solder it to an outside capacitor or resistor to re-create the old circuitry ... but in a *new* pathway that had never been used.

Our brain works in a very similar fashion. Imagine that the burnt circuitry is the pathway from a negative experience you had as a child. You had your first experience that triggered your first blown fuse, then other experiences started to accumulate and build on top of each other until you had a completely burned-out circuit board. This is one of the reasons doing affirmations will not be enough to repair burned-out circuitry. If your pathway is burned like that, there is no way you can repair it, so you have to create a *new* pathway and allow the brain to adapt to the new environment of change.

What this journal will assist you in doing is creating a new path. You've worked on yourself for many years, and now you can finally delete some of the things you've been holding onto.

First, let me tell you one thing: Always remember there is nothing wrong with you. You are enough. If you were told differently and you believed it, it's a lie! Your uniqueness starts from where you are.

Many of us have tried to heal our childhood. Many have tried forgiveness, affirmations, and other techniques, and maybe they provided some temporary relief, but in the end, failed to provide a long-term change.

What is needed is a reprogramming of your experiences, letting go of your old burned-out pathway. It is time to start with a new pathway. Whatever happened in your past already happened, and there is nothing, and I mean nothing, you can do today to change what happened. You will rarely get any apology from the person(s) who inflicted the experience on you.

Are you willing to let go of your old experiences and create a new pathway? Are you ready to choose and make new choices in your life using your own free will? Have you decided it's time to stop blaming, resenting, being angry, raging, and keeping yourself trapped in your old experiences?

If your answer is yes, this journaling process will program a new pathway. I call this process *taking responsibility for your own life.* If you've noticed, I did not say you were going to reprogram the old defective pathway. I simply said you will program a totally new pathway of your own choosing. When you decide to choose a new pathway or direction in your life, you're already giving yourself the permission to move in a new direction, and your mind will start to act according to your new choices, overriding the old burnt circuitry altogether. Just like the TV I was repairing, once the internal processor recognizes the flow of a new energy, it won't even notice that the old burnt pathway is no longer being used.

There is a specific way I'd like you to write in your journal. Are you ready?

First, if you are used to writing and reading from front to back, get ready for a change! You're now going to write from the back of this notebook to the front. If you are used to writing from back to front, then you will start from the front of this notebook and work toward the back.

Whatever direction you usually write in, you'll need to do the opposite. This makes a dramatic impact and shift for a new pathway that your brain hasn't been accustomed to. Once your brain gets used to it, it becomes a norm and your new pathway is already created.

Second, every sentence you write must begin with "I choose" in order to create your NEW YOU—the vision of yourself that has been put on the side for a long time. In Numerology, "I choose" is equal to 11. 11, which connects with the old Soul you are, with a vision to make a change in the world. That vision must always start with you first, before turning it over to humanity.

What is your new vision of the NEW YOU?

I stress that consistency is very important, and so what you must do every day for at least 90 days is the following:

▶ Write at least one page a day in the journal.

▶ Sit for fifteen minutes to read over what you wrote and notice in your body how that feels.

▶ Sit for fifteen minutes visualizing what you wrote in your mind so you can become familiar with it.

▶ After seven days of writing, do seven days of posting a picture that reflects what you desire and choose to have. Post one page a day of pictures.

▶ You had seven days of writing and seven days of pictures, for a total of fourteen days. On day fifteen, go back and reread what you wrote and see what you created in pictures.

- ▶ Go back to your writing of day one through seven. You can continue writing on the same desires you chose or choose a new desire. Think about what is needed for you today. Is it relationships? Health? Finances? What are you looking for in your life that you feel is missing or that you are always yearning for? Choose whatever you desire. You are building the new version of yourself. Define it as you want to define it. There are no limitations. Be open to your desires and a new vision of yourself.

- ▶ Repeat the above for a total of seven rounds of fifteen days each.

If you slip back into the old version of yourself, there is no need to beat yourself up. Be gentle and kind to yourself. You are worth it. You simply need to *acknowledge your slip*, then *embrace it* and *take action to choose what you desire*.

Remember …

- ▶ You can't be poor and rich at the same time. You've got to choose.

- You can't be sick and healthy at the same time. You've got to choose.

- You can't be struggling and abundant at the same time. You've got to choose.

- You can't be miserable and happy at the same time. You've got to choose.

Choose your desires. Choose!

No more blaming anyone for your life today. Today you can start to *wake up to a new you*™.

I learned to ask questions in a specific way when I studied with *Access Consciousness*™. There is no need to answer the questions yourself. Allow the Universe to bring the answer to you and to show you the way. I give a few examples below of sentences beginning with "I choose," followed by a question that you can pose to the Universe.

◆◆◆

I choose to be happy, joyful, and fulfilled, moving forward with total ease. What does it take for me to be happy, joyful, and fulfilled with total ease?

I choose to receive financial abundance with total ease. What does it take for me to receive financial abundance with total ease?

I choose to have a healthy body with ease. What does it take for me to receive a healthy body with total ease?

I choose to receive and have a flow of abundance of money from all directions with total ease. What does it take for me to receive and have a flow of abundance of money from all directions with total ease?

I choose to close all of the loopholes of my past and start my new life. What does it take to close all of the loopholes of my past and start my new life with total ease?

I choose to get my life back effortlessly with my new direction and desire. What does it take to get my life back effortlessly with my new direction and desire with total ease?

Now, go to the end of the journal and start writing, place some pictures, and choose to create your New You, your New Journey, and your New Desires.

Rewiring and reprogramming your subconscious is made easy for you. Wake up to a new you™ and choose your new desire. Whether you say no or yes to making a change, you are going to use the same energy. It is your call. Think about it! Choose wisely!

Happy writing and happy awakened NEW YOU!

DAY 7

DAY 6

DAY 5

DAY 4

DAY 3

DAY 2

DAY 1

DAY 7

DAY 6

DAY 5

DAY 4

DAY 3

DAY 2

DAY 1

DAY 7

DAY 6

DAY 5

DAY 4

DAY 3

DAY 2

DAY 1

DAY 7

DAY 6

DAY 5

DAY 4

DAY 3

DAY 2

DAY 1

DAY 7

DAY 6

DAY 5

DAY 4

DAY 3

DAY 2

DAY 1

DAY 7

DAY 6

DAY 5

DAY 4

_____

_____

_____

_____

_____

_____

_____

_____

_____

_____

_____

_____

_____

_____

_____

_____

_____

_____

_____

_____

DAY 3

DAY 2

DAY 1

DAY 7

DAY 6

DAY 5

DAY 4

DAY 3

DAY 2

DAY 1

DAY 7

DAY 6

DAY 5

DAY 4

DAY 3

DAY 2

DAY 1

DAY 7

DAY 6

DAY 5

DAY 4

DAY 3

DAY 2

DAY 1

DAY 7

DAY 6

DAY 5

DAY 4

DAY 3

DAY 2

DAY 1

DAY 7

DAY 6

DAY 5

DAY 4

DAY 3

DAY 2

DAY 1

DAY 7

DAY 6

DAY 5

DAY 4

DAY 3

DAY 2

DAY 1

DAY 7

DAY 6

DAY 5

DAY 4

DAY 3

DAY 2

DAY 1

DAY 7

DAY 6

DAY 5

DAY 4

DAY 3

DAY 2

DAY 1

Resources
For More information

Visit www.IChoose2Journal.com and sign up to receive additional support that will guide you on your journey with this book. You will receive messages, meditations, visualizations.

Also, visit my website for more information: www.SoulVisionAwakening.com

Events you might be interested in:

Consciously Living Your Life
3-Day Live Event in Vancouver, Canada
www.soulvisionawakening.com/consciously-living-your-destiny-life/

Online Programs:

1) **Vision Board Masterclass** (4 weeks)
   www.soulvisionawakening.com/vision-board-masterclass/

2) **Spiritual Council Masterclass** (6 weeks)
   www.soulvisionawakening.com/spiritual-council/

3) **Soul to Soul Connection Level 1** (12 weeks)
   Releasing and cutting the Soul Agreement
   https://www.soulvisionawakening.com/soul-to-soul-connection-level-1/

Attract the Right People Into Your Life and Clear Out Non-Serving Relationships

"If you don't make peace with your past, it will keep showing up in your present."
~ Wayne Dyer

4) **The New Frontier Healer Certification**
   Online Program on Blueprint Numerology
   https://www.soulvisionawakening.com/new-frontier-healer/

5) **Awakening Mastery for Masters** - 18 / 24
   Mentoring program including two certifications
   https://www.soulvisionawakening.com/awakening-mastery/

Meet Joseph P. Ghabi

When you hear the words mystic, master healer, spiritual teacher, or numerologist, Joseph may not fit the first picture that comes to mind.

Joseph is a former engineer, banker, and international sales manager. His past is packed with degrees and certifications given only to people of science and logic, yet Joseph's true gift appears in an area less frequented by typical scientists.

A master healer, an expert Blueprint Numerologist and spiritual leader, Joseph speaks on topics ranging from relationships and the Law of Attraction to life purpose and past histories. He is well known for his program *Soul To Soul Connection*, where he uses his gifts to help others free themselves and make peace with their past. As a psychosomatic therapist, and drawing upon his extensive knowledge of Numerology, Joseph developed Psychosomatic Numerology, which focuses on the relationship between one's emotions, mind, and body, in conjunction with Chakras and their connection with diseases.

Joseph's new gift recently showed up in the form of painting. He painted over 100 paintings just in his first 14 months. Now, he aligns his gift of healing with painting and meditation.

Joseph has earned several degrees, certifications, and diplomas studying subjects from engineering and computer programming to metaphysics and psychosomatic therapy.

Joseph is a #1 best-selling author for his book, *The Blueprint of Your Soul*, and has hosted his own radio shows, and he's now hosting a new podcast: *Numerology 4 Life*. When he speaks, Joseph is forceful and to the point. As a guest, producers love knowing his presence will light up the phone lines with curious callers seeking answers to their most pressing life problems. He's been featured in Lebanon, France, Canada, and the United States.

Joseph's mixed past is one of his greatest strengths. His wide range of educational, professional, and worldly experiences makes him a delight to listen to. He has a wealth of interesting stories to share and a profound ability to connect with people of many cultures, countries, and beliefs.

He lives in Vancouver with his son Robbie and daughter Tiffany.

Made in the USA
San Bernardino, CA
22 December 2019

61777724R00120